# Next to an Ant

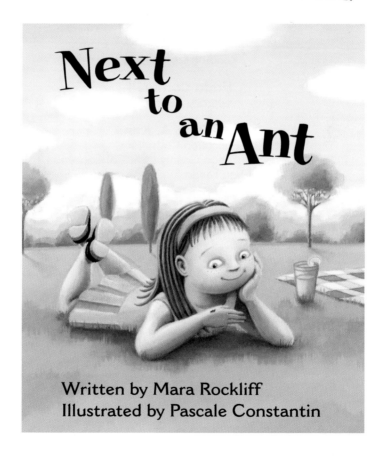

Written by Mara Rockliff
Illustrated by Pascale Constantin

Children's Press®
A Division of Scholastic Inc.
New York • Toronto • London • Auckland • Sydney
Mexico City • New Delhi • Hong Kong
Danbury, Connecticut

## For Cassidy
—M.R.

## In memory of lovely picnics on the mountain with Nathalie and Patrick
—P.C.

Reading Consultants

**Linda Cornwell**
Literacy Specialist

**Katharine A. Kane**
Education Consultant
(Retired, San Diego County Office of Education
and San Diego State University)

Library of Congress Cataloging-in-Publication Data
Rockliff, Mara.
  Next to an ant / written by Mara Rockliff ; illustrated by Pascale Constantin.
     p. cm. – (A Rookie reader)
Summary: A child compares the size of various items and discovers that she is the tallest of all.
  ISBN-10: 0-516-25903-2 (lib. bdg.)        0-516-26830-9 (pbk.)
  ISBN-13: 978-0-516-25903-1 (lib. bdg.)   978-0-516-26830-9 (pbk.)
  [1. Size—Fiction.] I. Constantin, Pascale, ill. II. Title. III.
Series.
PZ7.R5887Ne 2004
[E]—dc22

                                    2003018617

Next to an ant,
a berry is tall.

Next to a berry,
a snail is tall.

Next to a snail,
a mouse is tall.

Next to a mouse,
my shoe is tall.

Next to my shoe,
my cup is tall.

Next to my cup,
my ball is tall.

Next to my ball,
my basket is tall.

Next to my basket,
my puppy is tall.

Next to my puppy,
my brother is tall.

# And I?

I am the tallest one of all!

**A Rookie reader®**
Repetitive Text

## Read these other titles in *A Rookie Reader®* series:

Always Be Safe

Dirty Larry (Revised Edition)

I Do Not Want To

Joshua James Likes Trucks (Revised Edition)

Just a Little Different

Listen to Me (Revised Edition)

Rosa Loves to Read

Splat!

Who Is Coming?

For a complete title listing, visit our website.

**children's press®**
an imprint of
**◼ SCHOLASTIC**
www.scholastic.com/librarypublishing

U.S. $4.95

ISBN-13: 978-0-516-26830-9
ISBN-10: 0-516-26830-9
90000

9 780516 268309